Magic of Faith

MAGIC OF FAITH

The Groundbreaking Classic on the Creative Power of Thought

by Joseph Murphy

author of
The Power of Your Subconscious Mind

Abridged and Introduced
by Mitch Horowitz

THE CONDENSED CLASSICS LIBRARY™

MEDIA

Published by Gildan Media LLC
aka G&D Media.
www.GandDmedia.com

Magic of Faith was originally published in 1954
G&D Media Condensed Classics edition published 2019
Abridgement and Introduction copyright © 2019 by Mitch
Horowitz

FIRST PRINT AND EBOOK EDITION: 2019

Cover design by David Rheinhardt of Pyrographx

Interior design by Meghan Day Healey of Story Horse, LLC.

ISBN: 978-1-7225-0061-0

Contents

The Bible as Blueprint
By Mitch Horowitz

For Joseph Murphy the Bible was a metaphysical blueprint to the individual's self-development. In this regard, Murphy was similar to his contemporary and friend, the great mystic Neville Goddard. Late in life, Murphy told an interviewer that the two men, coming of age as writers and seekers in New York City in the 1930s—Murphy a recent transplant from Ireland and Neville from the West Indies—had the same teacher, a black-Jewish spiritual master named Abdullah.

In this vein, I am particularly struck by chapter three of this book, "Realizing Your Desire," in which Murphy sounds very much in harmony with Neville. Like his fellow seeker, Murphy taught that desire is God's voice speaking to you. "Desire pushes man,"

Murphy wrote, "it is the goad of action. It is behind all progress. Desire is really the cosmic urge in all of us, impelling us to go forward, onward, upward, and Godward."

Passages like this one helped me clarify my personal search. Mine is a path of aspiration. This divided me for many years. I wasn't sure how to truly practice the teaching, "Thy will be done." Murphy makes it clear that there is no "I" and "Thy"—all is One. The voice of higher forces reaches you through your wishes and desires, which are the impetus toward progress, achievement, and self-actualization. Murphy teaches you to trust your desires.

In a striking and daring passage, Murphy writes: "*Jesus* means your desire which, if realized, would be your savior. Jesus comes into your mind as an idea, desire, plan, purpose, vision, or some new undertaking."

In *Magic of Faith*, which Murphy wrote in 1954, nine years before his classic *The Power of Your Subconscious Mind,* Murphy, like Neville, highlighted the uses of Scripture as a symbolical and practical guidebook to understanding the creative potentials of your mind. Murphy also used case studies to drive home his points of application. The sum total of what he wrote can give you a larger, more epic sense of yourself and your possibilities.

Neville taught that the imagination is God. Murphy saw God functioning in us through the imagination. But the difference is minor. Both men believed that you, the individual, have far too small a sense of who you really are: a branch of the Divine clothed in flesh. Murphy wrote this book, distilled here to its essentials, to introduce you to that greater life. It is not outside of you. It is your very birthright.

CHAPTER I

The Song Of Triumph

Y ou sing the Song of God, or the mood of triumph, when you subjectively feel that you are that which your five senses tell you you are not; you are then God-intoxicated and seized with a Divine frenzy—a sort of mad joy.

Haven't you at times seen a person bubbling over with enthusiasm and intoxicated with joy? That person is singing the Song of God at that moment. "In thy presence *is* fulness of joy; at thy right hand *there are* pleasures for evermore."

The real You is a spiritual, eternal, perfect being. You are a living expression of God now. "I have said, Ye *are* Gods; and all of you are children of the most High."

When you pray, it is a romance with God or your Good. Your desire, when realized, brings you joy and peace. In order to realize the desire of your heart, which is depicted in *The Song of Solomon* as your beloved, you must woo it; let that desire of yours captivate, hold, and thrill you. Let it fire your imagination. You will always move in the direction of the desire that dominates your mind.

If you are saying to yourself, "I can't. It is too late now. I am too old, and I don't know the right people"— in other words if you are mentally feeding on all the reasons why you cannot do something, or be what you want to be, you are not making "thy flock to rest at noon."

At noon the sun casts no shadow; likewise, when you pray, you are not to permit any shadow of fear or doubt to cross your path, or deflect you from your goal or aim in life. The world of confusion shall be rejected, and you shall mentally eat of or meditate on the reality of your desire.

Once I talked to an alcoholic who said, "Don't say anything about this God-stuff to me. I don't want God. I want a healing." This man was deeply resentful toward a former wife who had remarried; moreover, he was full of grudges against several people. He needed the *doves' eyes,* which means he needed to see the truth that would give him peace of mind.

I asked him, "Will you pray with me now? All I ask is that you be sincere; if you are, you will experience an inner peace which passeth all human understanding."

He relaxed his body, and I said to him, "Imagine you are talking to the Invisible Presence within you—the Almighty Power which created the Cosmos. It can do all things. Say, 'Thank you, thank you, for this inner peace.' Say it over and over again."

After ten minutes in silent meditation, he was blinded by an interior, Inner Light. It seemed to come from the floor where he was. The whole room was flooded with Light!

He exclaimed, "All I see is Light! What's wrong?" Then he relaxed into sleep in my office, and his face did truly shine as the sun. He awakened in about fifteen minutes, and was completely at peace saying, "God truly is! God is!" This man had found his Beloved; It had *doves' eyes*.

As you fall asleep at night, tell your desire how fair it is, and how wonderful you would feel in realizing it. Begin to fall in love with your ideal. Praise it; exalt it. "Arise my Love!" Feel that you are what you want to be. Go to sleep in the consciousness of being or doing what you long to do.

I told a man in one of the islands one time "to sleep" on the idea of success. He was selling magazine subscriptions. He became a great success by following this procedure: I suggested that he think of success prior to sleep; i.e., what success meant to him; what he would do if he were successful. I told him to use his imagination; then as he was about to go to sleep, fall in love with the idea of success this way: Repeat the one word, "Success," over and over again. He should get into the mood of success; then fall off to sleep in the arms of his Everlasting Lover. Your Lover—your Divine Presence—will bring to pass whatever you accept as true. The conditions, experiences, and events of your life are called children of your mind.

You know when there is no longer any argument or doubt in your conscious or subconscious mind, your prayer is answered, because the two have agreed as touching upon it, and it is so.

I had a long talk with a man in England who had trouble with his leg. He had been confined to his home for nine months, and was unable to lean on his leg or walk. The first thing I did was to ask him what he would do if he were healed? He said, "I would again play polo, swim, golf, and climb the Alps which I used to do every year." That was the answer I was seeking.

I told him in the simplest way how to achieve the perfect use of his legs again. The first thing was to imagine he was doing the things he would do. I painted an imaginary picture for him. For fifteen or twenty minutes three times a day he sat in his study and imagined he was playing polo; he assumed the mental mood of actually performing the role of a polo player. He became the actor; an actor participates in the role.

Note carefully that he did not see himself playing polo; that would be an illusion. He *felt* himself playing polo. He actualized it by living the drama in his mind or *banquet house*.

At noon he would quiet the mind; still the body, and feel his Alpine clothes on him. He would feel and imagine he was climbing the Alps; he would feel the cold air on his face, and hear the voice of his old associates. He lived the drama and felt the naturalness and the tangibility of the rocks.

At night prior to sleep, before going into the Arms of his Beloved—His Deeper Self—he would play a game of golf. He would hold the club; touch the ball with his hand; put it in place, and tee off. He would swing his clubs, and delight in watching where the ball went.

Within two months this man's leg was healed. He did all the things he imagined he would do. The *idea* of climbing the Alps, plus the *desire* to play polo again, said to this man, "Arise, my love, my fair one, and come away," from your belief in a physical handicap; that is what he did.

The law of the subconscious is one of compulsion. When you subjectively feel you are swimming—for example, when you feel the chill of the water, and the naturalness of your various swimming strokes—you will sooner or later be compelled to swim. Whatever the handicap, whether fear or a physical condition, you will do what you subjectively felt you were doing.

Your desire, dream, ambition, goal, or aim is your savior! It is walking down the corridor of your mind, saying to you, "Arise, my love, and come away," and enjoy the good and glorious things of life.

No matter what the problem is, or its magnitude, you have really nothing to do but convince yourself of the truth that you are affirming. As quickly as you succeed in convincing yourself of the reality of your desire, results will automatically follow. Your subconscious mind will faithfully reproduce what you impregnated within it.

The Bible says, "Choose you this day whom ye will serve." You have the freedom to choose the tone, feeling, or mood you enter into. The manifestation of your feeling or conviction is the secret of your lover or subconscious mind. Your external actions are, therefore, determined by your subconscious beliefs and impressions.

Your thought and feeling determine your destiny. The knowledge of the truth is saying to you now, "The winter is past, the rain is over *and* gone." *The winter* represents that cold state when the seeds are frozen in the bosom of the earth and nothing is growing. The winter and all the seasons are in your mind.

Do everything from the standpoint of the One God and His Love. For instance, when you shop, pray before purchasing. Say, "God guides me in all my purchases." Say quietly to the saleslady or salesman, "God is prospering him."

Whatever you do, do it with love and good will. Pour out love, peace, and good will to all. Claim frequently that God's Love and Transcendent Beauty flow through all my thoughts, words, and actions. Make a habit of this. Fill your mind with the eternal verities; then you will see that "The flowers appear on the earth; the time of the singing of *birds* is come!" You will begin to *flower;* yes, you will begin to blossom forth.

When you go into a home, and you see confusion, quarrelling, and strife, you will realize within yourself, that the peace of God reigns supreme in the minds and hearts of all those in this house; you will see the flower of peace made manifest and expressed.

Where you see financial lack and limitation, you will realize the infinite abundance and wealth of God forever flowing, filling up all the empty vessels, and leaving a Divine surplus. As you do this, you will live in the garden of God where only orchids and all beautiful flowers grow; for only God's ideas circulate in you.

Tennyson said, "Speak to Him, thou, for He hears, and Spirit with Spirit can meet—closer is He than breathing, and nearer than hands and feet."

One time as a boy I was lost in the woods. I sat down under a tree, and remembered a prayer that starts with, "Our Father, He will show us the way; let us be quiet, and He will lead us." I quietly repeated, "Father, lead us."

A wave of peace came over me, which I can still recall. *The voice of the turtle dove* became real. *The turtle dove* is intuition which means being taught from within. An overpowering feeling came over me to go in a certain direction as if I were being pushed ahead. Two of the boys came with me; the others did not. We were led out of that thick jungle, as if by an Unseen Hand.

Great musicians have listened and heard the music within; they wrote down what they heard inwardly. In meditation Lincoln listened to the principle of liberty; Beethoven heard the principle of harmony.

If you are intensely interested in the principle of mathematics, you are loving it; as you love it, it will reveal all its secrets to you.

Jesus heard *the voice of the turtle dove* when he said, "Peace, I leave with you; my peace I give unto you; not as the world giveth, give I unto you. Let not your heart be troubled; neither let it be afraid." How wonderful you will feel as you drink in these words and fill your mind with their therapeutic potency.

Job heard *the voice of the turtle* when he said, "Acquaint now thyself with Him, and be at peace." "Thou wilt keep *him* in perfect peace, *whose* mind is stayed *on thee:* because he trusteth in thee." "For God is not *the author* of confusion, but of peace."

If you want guidance, claim Infinite Intelligence is guiding you now; It will differentiate Itself as right action for you. You will know you have received the answer, for *the dove of peace* will whisper in your ear, "Peace be still." You will know the Divine answer, for you will be at peace, and your decision will be right.

A girl recently was wondering whether to accept a position in New York for considerably more money or remain in Los Angeles in her present position. At night as she went to sleep, she asked herself this question, "What would be my reaction if I had made the right decision now?" The answer came to her, "I would feel wonderful. I would feel happy having made the right decision." Then she said, "I will act as though I had made the right decision," and she began to say, "Isn't it wonderful! Isn't it wonderful!" over and over again, as a lullaby, and lulled herself to sleep in the feeling, "It is wonderful."

She had a dream that night, and the voice in the dream said, "Stand still! Stand still!" She awakened immediately, and knew of course that was *the voice of the turtle dove*—the voice of intuition.

The fourth dimensional-self within her can see ahead; it knows all and sees all; it can read the minds of the owners of the business in the east. She remained in her present position. Subsequent events proved the truth of her Inner Voice; the Eastern concern went into bankruptcy. "I the Lord will make myself known unto him in a vision, *and* will speak unto him in a dream."

By realizing and knowing these qualities and attributes of God are being expressed through you, and that you are a channel for the Divine, every atom of your being begins to dance to the rhythm of the Eternal God. Beauty, order, harmony, and peace appear in your mind, body, and business world as you feed among the lilies; you feel your oneness with God, Life, and God's Infinite Riches. You are married to your Beloved, for you are now married to God; you are a bride of the Lord (I AM). From this moment forward you will bring forth children of your Beloved; they will bear the image and likeness of their Father and Mother.

The *father* is God's idea; the *mother* is the emotionalizing of the idea, and its subjective embodiment. From that union of idea and feeling come forth your health, abundance, happiness, and inner peace.

When you go to sleep tonight, forgive everyone, and imagine and feel your desire is fulfilled. Become absolutely and completely indifferent to all thought of failure, because you now know the law. As you accept the end, you have, as Thomas Troward so beautifully stated, willed the means to the realization of the end. As you are about to enter sleep, galvanize yourself into the feeling of being or having your desire. Your mental acceptance or your feeling as you go to sleep is the request you make of your Beloved; then She looks at your request (conviction in the subconscious mind), and being the Absolute Lover, she must give you what you asked.

When you pray, accept as true what your reason and five senses deny and reject. Remain faithful to your idea by being full of faith every step of the way. When your consciousness is fully qualified with the acceptance of your desire, all the fear will go away. Trust in the reality of your ideal or desire until you are filled full of the feeling of being it; then *the day will break and all shadows will flee away.* Yes, the answer to your prayer will come, and light up the heavens of your mind bringing you peace.

No matter what the problem is, how acute, dark, or hopeless things seem to be, turn now to God, and say, "How is it in God and Heaven?" The answer will softly steal over your mind like the dew from heaven: "All is peace, joy, bliss, perfection, wholeness, harmony, and beauty"; then reject the evidence of your senses, and *feed among the lilies of God and Heaven,* such as peace, harmony, joy, and perfection. Realize what is true of God must be true of you and your surroundings. Continue in this abiding trust and faith in God "until the day breaks and the shadows flee away."

Chapter II

The Practice of
the Presence of God

"Whither shall I go from thy Spirit? or whither shall I flee from thy presence? If I ascend up into heaven, thou ART THERE, If I take the wings of the morning, AND dwell in the uttermost parts of the sea; Even there shall thy hand lead me, and thy right hand shall hold me."

This one hundred and thirty ninth Psalm is one of the most beautiful Psalms in the Bible. It is a matchless, priceless gem of truth. The language of this Psalm is unsurpassed for beauty and elegance. David's marvelous conception of the Omnipresence of God was found in this passage.

The religion outlined in the Bible is the practice of the Presence of God. To understand and to intelligently practice this truth, you will find is the way to health, harmony, peace, and spiritual progress. The practice of the Presence is powerful beyond imagination. Let us not overlook it, because of its utter simplicity.

The first step is to realize that God is the Only Power. The next thing to become aware of is that all things—no matter what they are—represent God in manifestation. The whole world is God in infinite differentiation, as God never repeats Himself; this is the whole story, and the greatest of all truths. It is really the all-inclusive, all-encompassing truth.

I know many students who sit down for five or ten minutes every day, and meditate on the fact that God is the Only Presence and the Only Power. They let their thoughts dwell on this profound truth; they look at it from all angles; then they begin to think that every person they meet is an expression of God; that in fact everything they see is God made manifest; it is God dramatizing Himself for the joy of expressing Himself. As they do this, they find their whole world changing; they experience better health; outer conditions improve, and they are possessed of a new vitality and energy.

Your whole world will change as you really begin to see God in everything and in everyone. "For thou shalt be in league with the stones of the field: and the beasts of the field shall be at peace with thee. And thou shalt know that thy tabernacle *shall* be in peace." This means that the man who begins to see God everywhere, and who follows and practices the good, will not be afraid of anything. As a matter of fact the whole world will be his friend, and everything will extend the offer of help whether animate, or what the world calls inanimate.

The only way to magnify the Presence of God in the eyes of others is to radiate at all times the sunlight of God's Love. Love God or Truth, and you will be under a Divine compulsion for good. You cannot go wrong. You will find that you will never make any real mistake or a wrong choice. Love of all things good, or of the truth, is really the touch of Midas.

In a building the superstructure depends upon the foundation. Let *your* foundation be God and Him alone. You are always practicing the Presence of God when you activate your mind with true ideas, which heal and strengthen you. Your mind needs constant cleansing, disciplining, and direction. By practicing the Presence of God, you are constantly cleansing your mind; this is prayer.

Think all day long from the standpoint of the One God about every person and every situation you meet. Pray at work by realizing God is your partner, and God is in action through all your associates.

Pray driving your car, by realizing the vehicle is God's idea moving from point to point freely, joyously, and lovingly.

Pray when you go into a store by realizing God directs your purchases, that God is prospering the clerk who waits on you, and that the store is being governed and directed by God's Wisdom.

Let prayer be the orderly, right way of doing everything. Practice the Golden Rule in all your transactions; then you are writing God's Law in your heart.

It is essential for you to get the right concept and understanding of God. Have you meditated? or have you asked yourself what God is? Your concept of God molds, fashions, and shapes your whole future. Your real belief about God is of supreme importance. It is done unto you as you believe. If you say and believe God is the only Presence, the only Power, Infinitely Good, Perfect, Boundless Love, and Limitless Life, your whole life will be transformed.

If you say, "Oh, I do not know what I think of God; my thoughts are confused and muddled," confusion will reign in your life. It does not really matter whether you call God: Reality, Infinite Intelligence, Being, Life, Allah, or Brahma; the real Name of God, in so far as you are concerned, is your concept or your belief about God.

A man said to me one time, "I believe in God, and that is all that matters." I asked him, "But tell me, what sort of God do you really believe in?" He said, "I believe in the laws of nature." That was his idea of God, and he cannot transcend this belief. He is subject to that belief, thereby limiting his Inner Powers. He had no idea that God was his own Life, that he could contact this Presence with his thought, that he could be guided, and that he could heal his body by prayer. He was bound by his limited belief about God. Many have said to me that God is some kind of a man in the skies—a sort of a glorified man. Others say and believe there are three persons in God. You will always manifest the result of your belief. If you believe that God is some sort of a tyrannical, inscrutable being living in the skies, ready to judge and punish you for your mistakes and violations of man-made laws and religious taboos, you are bound by that belief, and you cause pain, misery, guilt complexes, and so forth. This is why Phineas Quimby said, "Man is belief expressed."

Your concept of God enters into all departments of your life; it is bound to have its effect upon you. God is Life, and Life seeks to express Itself as Love, Light, Truth, and Beauty. Life cannot wish death, sickness, or disease. To say that Life wishes death would be a violation of its own nature. Life cannot have a tendency toward limitation of any kind. Life is a Oneness, a Wholeness, a Unity, and It seeks to express that Unity in the formed universe.

In order to practice the Presence, you must do the will of God. What does this mean? *The will of God* must always be the nature of God. You can rest assured the will of God must always be something wonderful and glorious. "His name shall be called Wonderful, Counsellor, The Mighty God, The Everlasting Father, The Prince of Peace."

If your desire, idea, or intention is constructive, if it will bless others, and if it is in keeping with the universal principle of harmony, your will or desire is God's will. Your desire for wealth, true place, abundance, security, and better living conditions conforms to the will or tendency of Life or God.

Life is forever seeking to express Itself through you along higher levels. Enthrone in your mind the concept that God is the Only Presence, the Only Power, and that God is Infinitely Good and Perfect. Think of some of God's qualities and attributes, such as Boundless Love, Infinite Intelligence, Indescribable Beauty, Omnipotence, Omniscience, and Omnipresence. Believe these truths about God, and your whole life will change. You will begin to express more and more God-like qualities every day. Believe that God is All Life, All Love, All Truth, and All Beauty; accept It in the same way as you accept the sun in the heavens each morning; then you will find a great sense of peace and goodwill stealing over your mind and heart.

Do you believe in a vengeful, capricious, anthropomorphic Deity who sends sickness, trials, and tribulation to you? Watch the effect of such a belief. If you do, you will be like the man who said to me one time, "God sent this arthritis to me for a good purpose, and I suppose I must just bear it." This is superstition; such an attitude of mind has no foundation. He had arthritis for fifteen years, and he could not overcome it.

When this man with arthritis got a new concept of God, and he learned to forgive those whom he deeply resented, by realizing the Love of God was dissolving in his mind and body everything unlike Itself, he was healed, even though it took some months. This man's concept of God worked out, and made Itself manifest in his body according to his belief.

It is not your theoretical belief about God that manifests itself, but it is your real, deep, subconscious belief.

There are people who forget to practice the Presence when a lawsuit or verdict goes against them. Even though the judge rendered a verdict which seems unjust to you, continue to believe that it is God in action, and that there is a Divine, harmonious solution for all concerned; the matter will come right in due season. You cannot lose; you can only win by practicing the Presence.

God is Pure Spirit, Infinite Mind, and Infinite Intelligence. The Bible calls the Name of God, "I AM," meaning Pure, Unconditioned Being. No one can, of course, define God, for God is Infinite, but there are certain Truths which the illumined of all ages have perceived as true of God, and that is why the Bible says, "I AM THAT I AM." What is "I AM?" It is your True Being—your Real Self; nobody can say, "I AM," for you. That is the Presence of God in you, and your Real Identity. Whatever you affix to "I AM," and believe, you become. Always claim, "I am strong, powerful, radiant, happy, joyous, illumined, and inspired;" then you are truly practicing the Presence, for all these qualities are true of God.

When you say, "I am weak," "I am inferior," "I am no good," you are denying God in the midst of you, and lying about Him.

Brother Lawrence of the 17th century was a monk. He was a saintly man, and wholly devoted to God. The book entitled *The Practice of the Presence of God* reveals a great humility, simplicity, and a mystic touch with God. "To do the will of God was," as he said, "his whole business." Brother Lawrence practiced the Presence when washing the dishes or scrubbing the floor. His attitude was that it was all God's work. His consciousness and awareness of the Divine Presence was no less when employed in the kitchen, than when he was before the altar. The way to God was to Brother Lawrence through the heart and through Love. His superiors marveled at the man who, though only educated to the point of reading and writing, could express himself with such beauty and profound wisdom. It was the Voice of God within him that prompted all his sayings.

This is how he daily practiced God's Holy Presence: He said in effect, "I have put myself in Your Keeping; it is Your Business I am about, and so everything will be all right." How beautiful! How simple, yet how soul-stirring is this prayer! He said the only sorrow he could experience would be the loss of the sense of God's Presence, but he never feared that, being wholly aware of God's Love and Absolute Goodness.

In his early life he feared he would be damned; this torture of his mind persisted for four years; then he saw the whole cause of this negativity was lack of faith in God; seeing that, he was freed and entered into a life of continual joy.

Begin now to practice the Presence by keeping your eyes on God, or all things Good, by seeing God in everyone you meet, and by constantly affirming, "It is God in action in all departments of my life." Calmly trust God's Holy Presence to lead you to green pastures and still waters. Love the Truth with a love that leaves no room for care or doubt. No matter what your work may be, as you go to your business say, "God walks and talks in me. I rely on God's guidance and wisdom completely." Give thanks for the perfect day. Do as Brother Lawrence suggests, whenever your attention wanders away on fear or doubt, bring it back to the contemplation of His Holy Presence.

To secure and know the life of peace and joy, school yourself daily to have an intimate, loving, familiar, humble conversation with God all day long. In this way you will draw upon God's grace abundantly. You shall become illumined by an Inner Light, and you will behold the inner vision of God, your Beloved.

Case Histories

CASE HISTORY NUMBER ONE

This interesting case from my files may bless many of you. This man invested a large sum of money in a certain organization. He had a very high regard for the two men who were active partners in this business. They appropriated the money that he gave them for themselves, and a little later they went into bankruptcy. He was very bitter and resentful, because he had practically put his life's savings into this venture. He was also ill, due to the hatred in his heart.

I explained to this man that resentment is never justified, and that many people make investments in land, stocks, bonds, etc., and have lost their money, but that it is absurd to blame the broker or the real estate man, because we erred in judgment. In a great measure this man's resentment was caused by a feeling of guilt for his own mistake, which he refused to admit. He was blaming the other men by an active resentment for his own shortcoming and failure. He prayed his way through it by the practice of His Presence in this way: "I now radiate love and goodwill to these two men. I humbly, sincerely, and honestly wish for them God's guidance, inner peace, and Divine Love. I wish for each one of them: prosperity, success, and a richness of life. It is God in action in all departments of their life. I mean this; I am sincere. My mind is now clear, clean, poised, serene, and expectant of happiness. God is guiding me in all ways. Nobody can take happiness, peace, or wealth away from me. I am one with God, and my business is God's Business. I am now minding my own business. The money I gave these men comes back to me in peace and harmony." He prayed like this night and morning, and during the day when hateful thoughts would come, he would say, "God is with me now."

In two weeks he was at peace with the world. All the resentful thoughts were burned up in his deeper mind; they were withered away by realizing God in action in his own life, and the life of those whom he said wronged him. A relative died in the interim, and a most interesting thing happened: He was bequeathed the exact amount he lost in that business venture. "For as the heavens are higher than the earth, so are my ways higher than your ways."

CHAPTER III

Realizing Your Desire

Desire is the power behind all action. We could not lift our hand or walk unless we had the desire or urge to move. Desire is the gift of God. As Browning said, "Tis thou, God, who giveth, 'tis I who receive."

It is man who receives—not a few of the gifts of life, but all of them! "Son thou art ever with me, and all that I hath is thine." All things whatsoever the Father hath are mine. *Our Father* holds within Himself all things we require, such as peace, harmony, abundance, guidance, joy, and infinite expression. We must grow unceasingly. We can never exhaust the Infinite Storehouse.

Let us realize a few simple truths: It is due to desire that we jump out of the way of an oncoming bus. The reason we do this is because we have a basic desire to preserve our life. Self-preservation is the first law of nature.

By example, the farmer plants seed due to his desire to attain food for himself and his family. Man builds airplanes due to his desire to collapse time and space. Similar illustrations are found throughout our whole course of life.

Desire pushes man; it is the goad of action. It is behind all progress. Desire is really the cosmic urge in all of us, impelling us to go forward, onward, upward, and Godward.

Desire is the angel of God—the messenger of the Divine—saying to each one of us, "Come on up higher."

Desire is behind all progress. It is the push of life. We find that we follow the desire that captivates and holds our attention. All of us find ourselves moving in the direction of the idea that dominates our mind for the time being.

Desire is an angel of God, telling us of something which, if accepted by us, will make our life fuller and happier. *The greater the expected benefit from the desire, the stronger is our desire.* Where there is no expected benefit, gain, or advancement accruing, there is no desire; consequently no action is found.

"I am alpha and omega, the beginning and the end, saith the Lord." Our ideal murmuring in our hearts is the alpha; in order that it become the omega, we must enter into the feeling that it is ours *now,* and walk the earth knowing that it is so.

Failure to realize our desire over a long period of time results in frustration and unhappiness. I have talked to many men in different parts of the country; their frequent complaint is that for years they have tried in vain to attain a certain ideal or position in life, and that they have failed miserably. They did not know that the desire to be, to do, and to have was the Still Small Voice speaking to them, and all that was necessary was for them to say, "Yes, Father, I accept and believe it"; then walk the earth knowing that, "It is done."

It is foolish to blame or accuse others, as we must realize that others are witnesses telling us who we are— "As within, so without." If there is discord within, there will be discord without. If we dwell in a mood of lack and limitation, others must come and testify to our lack.

I knew a woman in London one time, and on three occasions her purse was snatched from her by a thief in the tube of London; she was a wealthy woman. The explanation for this is that she was living in the fear of having her purse stolen; this was really an expectancy. "What I fear most has come upon me."

The mood, feeling, or conviction in which we walk determines the movements and actions of others towards us. In the eleventh chapter of Mark it says, "All things whatsoever ye shall ask in prayer, believe that ye receive them, and ye shall receive them."

The word *whatsoever* in the above quotation means anything you wish; it is all inclusive. There are no specific conditions set forth; you do not have to be a church-goer, or belong to a certain creed, or make any sacrifices. "I rejoice not in the sacrifices of man, not by power, not by might, but by the spirit saith the Lord." "For what purposes is the multitude of thy sacrifices. I am full of the blood of rams and the fat of beast, I rejoice not in the blood of rams or he goats." The only requisite is to believe that you have it now, or that you are the being you long to be.

Believe means to live in the state of being it; this means a complete mental acceptance where there is no longer any doubt or question in your mind. This is the state of consciousness called "a conviction." All other procedures as cited by Isaiah are foolishness and superstition. The only prerequisite is to believe that you have received; then comes the manifestation of your ideal.

We grow through desire. It is desire that pushes us forward, for it is the cosmic urge.

Let us realize that we are all channels of the Divine—individualizations   of   God-consciousness. The desire that lingers in your heart, that murmurs quietly—perhaps it has been there for months making itself known to you—is the Voice of God speaking to you, telling you to come on up higher— to arise and shine. Maybe you have looked around you and said to yourself, "What chance have I?" "Mary can, but I can't." "Perhaps, someday!" "It is just wishful thinking, etc." Have many such expressions come to your mind? Remember it is your five senses and worldly reason arguing with your Higher Self. We must remember that in prayer we always shut out the evidence of our senses and reason, plus everything that contradicts or denies what we truly want; then, as Jesus commands, we go within; shut the door, and pray to our Father in secret; the Father who seeth in secret will reward thee openly. Let us now proceed to enter into this Secret Place, and perform the spiritual, creative act in our own mind.

Sit down in an armchair, relax, and let go. Practice the Nancy School technique by getting into a drowsy, meditative state, a state of effortless effort, wherein effort is reduced to a minimum.

By example if you want to be a singer on the radio, imagine you are before a microphone; the microphone is now in front of you, and you see the imaginary audience; you are the actor. ("Act as though I am, and I will be.") You *feel* yourself into the situation; you are singing now (in your imagination); enter into the joy of it; feel the thrill of accomplishment! Continue to do this in your imagination until it begins to feel natural for you; then go off to sleep. If you have succeeded in planting your desire in your subconscious mind, you will feel a great sense of peace and satisfaction when you awaken. An interesting thing will have happened: You will have no further desire to pray about it, because it is fixed in consciousness. The reason for this is that the creative act has been finished, and you are at rest.

After true prayer when you have reached an inner conviction, there steals over you a sense of inner peace, calm, and certitude which tells you, "All is well." This is called *the sabbath* in the Bible, or period of stillness, or rest; it is the interval that elapses between the subjective realization of your desire and its manifestation. The manner of manifestation is not known to you; that is the secret of the subjective. "My ways are past finding out."

The answer or manifestation comes as a thief in the night. You know a thief comes when you least expect him; there is always an element of surprise; perhaps when you are sound asleep, the thief will come. If you sit up watching and waiting for the intruder, he will not come. Likewise we must go about our daily business, and the moment we think not, the answer will come. You are now at peace, made whole so to speak. You do not have to assist this Infinite Intelligence; It is All Powerful. It would be foolish to try to add power to Power.

The trouble with many people is this: When they pray, they are tense, anxious, and impatient. They say, "I wonder when it will come?" Others say, "Why has it not happened yet?"

If I say, "Why?" it means I am anxious and lack faith. If I *know* a thing is true, I do not question my prayer. Let us remember, therefore, anytime we ask, "Why?" to ourself or another, it means we have not reached a conviction within ourselves.

When we possess something in consciousness, we do not seek it; we have it! Another point I want to stress here is: When the student questions, "How will it come?" he shows lack of faith and conviction.

Case Histories

CASE HISTORY NUMBER TWO

Several years ago the author was lecturing in the Park Central Hotel in New York City. A man spoke to me at the end of the meeting saying, "I desire desperately to go to Pittsburgh, and I have no money."

I said to him, "Did you hear the lecture?" He said, "Yes, but—." I told him to ignore the doubts in his mind. We made a simple statement of truth together in that lovely lecture room. The statement was, "I am now at home in Pittsburgh with my people. All is peace and harmony." He was at home with them during those few minutes of silence in his imagination and feeling.

He phoned me later saying, "I went to the restaurant, and a man who sat next to me said, "You know I am driving to Pittsburgh. I would love to have someone share in the driving; I would pay him also. Do you know anyone? You look like a mechanic." This was the way Infinite Intelligence answered this man's prayer.

Chapter IV

The Magic of Faith

The purpose of this chapter is to teach you the spiritual truth of your dominion and freedom. "In all thy ways acknowledge him, and he shall direct thy paths." (Prov. 3:6). "I will lift up mine eyes unto the hills, from whence cometh my help." (Psm. 121:1).

In the above verse from Proverbs you are told to acknowledge the Infinite Intelligence within you, and that It shall direct you in all ways. The answer to your problem will come when you turn in faith and recognition to the Divine Principle within.

It was Shakespeare who said, "Our doubts are traitors, making us lose the good we oft might win, by fearing to attempt." Fear holds us back. *Fear* is a lack of faith in God or the Good.

A man told me one time that he was a member of a sales force for a large chemical organization which had two hundred men in the field. The sales manager died, and the vice president offered him the position; however he turned it down. He realized later that the only reason he rejected the offer was due to fear. He was afraid to attempt the responsibility. This man lacked faith in himself and his Inner Power. He hesitated, and the wonderful opportunity passed him by.

This salesman came to me for consultation, and I learned he was condemning himself, which was like a destructive, mental poison. In place of condemnation, he began to realize that there were other opportunities. I explained to him that faith is a way of thinking, a positive mental attitude, or a feeling of confidence that what you are praying for will come to pass.

For example, you have faith that the sun will rise tomorrow. You have faith that the seed you deposited in the ground will grow. The electrician has faith that electricity will respond to his proper use of it. A scientist has an idea for an ediphone; he proceeds to bring it to pass by having faith in the execution of the invisible idea.

Opportunity is always knocking at your door. The desire for health, harmony, peace, and prosperity is knocking at your door now. Perhaps you are offered a promotion; are you going to act like Peter of old who walked on the waters? ("And when Peter was come down out of the ship, he walked on the water, to go to Jesus. But when he saw the wind boisterous, he was afraid; and beginning to sink, he cried, Lord, save me.")

Besides being historical, this drama of Peter and Jesus takes place in your own mind. *Peter* means faith, perseverance, and determination. *Jesus* means your desire, which, if realized, would be your savior. Jesus comes into your mind as an idea, desire, plan, purpose, vision, or some new undertaking. The realization of your dreams, plans, or purpose would bring you and others great satisfaction and inner joy; this would be your Jesus. You must now call Peter, which is faith in the God-Power to bring all things to pass. Look at Peter and Jesus as dramatizations of the power of truth within you.

Oftentimes as you attempt something new—for example, a new position—doubt comes into your mind; this is *Peter* in you looking at the *boisterous wind and sinking*. This represents the impingement in your mind of the belief in failure, lack, and limitation.

You must cremate, burn up, and destroy that negative thought immediately. Doubt and fear hold men in bondage of sickness and failure. These false concepts cause you to vacillate, waver, equivocate, and hesitate to go ahead. The way to overcome is to increase your faith and awareness of your deep, spiritual potencies. Be like Peter; he succeeded, because he went forward; he had faith and confidence, knowing he would succeed.

A general in the field cannot afford to vacillate and waver on the battlefield. He has to come to a decision. Failure to come to a decision, plus a constant wavering in the mind, leads to a nervous breakdown and mental confusion. When you find yourself being pulled two ways that is a sign of doubt and fear.

Your good comes to you in the form of your desire. If you are sick, you wish health. If you are poor, you desire wealth. If you are full of fear, you desire faith and confidence. Jesus comes as your desire walking down the streets of your mind.

Ideas are our lords and masters. Ideas govern and rule us. The dominant idea that you now entertain is your lord; it generates its own emotion. Emotions compel you to express them. The dominant idea of success enthroned in the mind generates its own mood or feeling. This feeling compels you to right action, so that whatever you do under the mood of faith and confidence will be successful. The desire or idea of yours now is your lord. Mentally appropriate your desire, kiss it, love it, let it captivate your mind; feel the reality of it.

Is your desire lofty, inspiring, and wonderful enough to lead you forward? This ideal of yours is real, just the same as the idea of a radio was real in the mind of the inventor; or the idea of an automobile was real in the mind of Ford; or the idea of a house is real in the mind of an architect. It is not idle fancy or a daydream.

Peter is within you; i.e., *Peter* is faith, perseverance, stick-to-it-iveness, and an abiding trust in an Almighty Power that responds to man's thought and belief. This Formless Awareness within you takes the form of your belief and conviction. It is really all things to all men. It is strength to you, if you need strength. It is guidance, if you need guidance. It is food and health also.

All great scientists, mystics, artists, poets, and inventors are gifted or possessed by an abiding faith and trust in the Invisible Powers within.

As you read this, turn your desire or request over to the subjective mind within you, acknowledging in your heart it has the answer and the "know how" of accomplishment, and that its ways are past finding out. When you are relaxed and peaceful, you will know you have succeeded in impregnating your deeper mind. Signs follow; the wave of peace is the sign; this is inner conviction. You now walk above all the waters of confusion, chaos, and false beliefs, because in a little while what you felt as true will be experienced.

Case Histories

CASE HISTORY NUMBER THREE

I visited a man in prison a few months ago. The first thought in his mind was freedom; this is symbolized in the Bible as Jesus walking on the waters of your mind. This prisoner was very bitter and cynical. I explained to him that he had placed himself in prison by his actions, which were contrary to the golden rule. He was living in a psychological prison of hatred and envy. He changed his mental attitude by calling forth Peter, which was his faith in an Almighty Power to bring to pass the cherished desire of his heart.

I gave detailed instruction to this prisoner. He began to pray for those he hated by saying frequently, "God's love flows through them, and I release them." He began to do this many times a day. At night prior to sleep, he imagined himself home with his family. He would feel his little daughter in his arms and hear her voice saying, "Welcome, daddy." All this was done in his imagination. After awhile he made this so real, natural, and vivid, that it became a part of him. He had impregnated the subconscious with the belief in freedom.

Another interesting thing happened; he had no further desire to pray for his freedom; this was a sure psychological sign to him that he had embodied the desire for freedom subjectively. He was at peace, and though he was behind bars, he knew subjectively that he was free. It was an inner knowing. You no longer seek that which you have. Having realized his desire subjectively, he had no further desire to pray about it.

A few weeks passed and this young man was liberated from prison. Friends came to his rescue, and through the proper channels, the door was opened to him for a new life.

CHAPTER V

Steps to Happiness

Happiness is a state of consciousness. Faith and fear are moods of the soul. Your faith is a joyous expectancy of the best. Fear comes to challenge your faith in God or the Good. You must look upon fear as man's ignorance or his false beliefs which try to overcome his conviction in the good.

Never entertain or accept the suggestions of sickness, weakness, or failure. If you listen to negative suggestions and become fearful, begin to affirm the Truths of God, such as Love, Peace, Joy, etc. Know that thought and feeling are the causes of conditions and experiences.

Fear is based on the false beliefs that there are other powers, and that external things and conditions can hurt you. Fear must leave you, because it has nothing to sustain it; there is no reality behind it; its claims are false. Come back to the simple truth: "Only your thought has power over you, and the One Almighty Power now moves on your behalf, because your thoughts are in tune with the Infinite One."

I met a farmer one time on the west coast of Ireland. I lived in his house for a few days. He seemed to be always happy and joyful. I asked him to tell me his secret of happiness. His answer was, "It is a habit of mine to be happy." This is the whole story! Prayer is a habit; happiness is likewise a habit.

There is a phase in the Bible: "Choose ye this day whom ye will serve." You have the freedom *to choose* happiness; this may seem extraordinarily simple—and it is. Perhaps this is why people stumble over the way to happiness; they do not see the simplicity of the key to happiness.

Perhaps you say to yourself, "Business is bad. It is going to get worse." Furthermore, you may say to yourself, "The worst is yet to come!" If you have this attitude of mind the first thing in the morning, you will attract all these experiences to you, and you will be very unhappy.

On the other hand you can choose happiness. This is how you do it: When you open your eyes in the morning, say to yourself, "All things work together for good to them that love God." Remember that in all languages God and Good are synonymous.

Love is an emotional attachment. Continue to become attached to the good in the morning in this way: Look out the window, and say, "This is God's day for me. I am Divinely guided all day long. Whatever I do will prosper. I cast the spell of God around me. I walk in His Light. Whenever my attention wanders away from God or the Good, I will immediately bring it back to the contemplation of God and His Holy Presence. I am a spiritual magnet attracting to myself all things that bless and prosper me. I am going to be a wonderful success in all my undertakings today. I am definitely going to be happy all day long."

Start each day in this manner; then you are choosing happiness, and you will be a radiant, joyous person.

You can experience nothing outside your own mentality. Your dominant, mental mood is the way you think and feel inside about yourself, others, and the world in general. What is your present mental attitude? How do you feel inside? Are you worried, confused, angry, or concerned about other people's actions? If you are, you are not happy, because you are dwelling mentally on limitation.

Begin to anchor your mind on thoughts of peace, success, and happiness; this is really prayer. Do this frequently; then you will be like the Irish farmer who said, "It is a habit of mine to be happy." Your dominant mental attitude rules and governs all your experiences; therefore nothing can come into your world but the out-picturing of your mental attitude. Love all things good, and even your so-called "enemies" will be constrained to do you good.

Oftentimes you read in psychological and metaphysical literature that the world you behold is the world you are; this means you can control your relationship with the world. The world you really live in is a mental world of thoughts, feelings, sensations, and beliefs. As a matter of fact every person, circumstance, and experience you meet becomes a thought in your mind. How you mentally feel and react to life and conditions depend on what you believe about life and things in general. If your knowledge about life and the world is false, you can be very unhappy. If you have true knowledge and the right ideas, you can control your emotional reactions to life and have inner peace.

I knew a woman in England who had rheumatism for twenty years. She would pat herself on the knee, and say, "My rheumatism is bad today. I can't go out; my rheumatism keeps me miserable." This dear, elderly lady got a lot of attention from her son, daughter, and the neighbors. She really wanted her rheumatism; she enjoyed her "misery," as she called it. This person did not really want to be happy.

I suggested a curative procedure given in the Bible. I wrote down some biblical verses, and said if she gave her attention to these truths, she would be healed, but she was not interested. There seems to be a peculiar, mental streak in many people, whereby they seem to enjoy being miserable and sad.

Jesus said, "If you know these things, happy are ye if ye do them." "We should become as little children." The reason for this is that a child is happy, because it is close to God. The child knows intuitively where to find happiness. You do not have to become old, dull, crotchety, petulant, and cantankerous; neither do you have to become jaded and depressed in spirit. The simple truths of life, and not the opinions of man, produce and generate happiness within us. There are a great number of people trying to buy happiness through the purchase of radios, television sets, automobiles, and a home in the country, but happiness cannot be purchased or procured that way.

The Kingdom of God is within you, and the kingdom of happiness is in your thought and feeling. Too many people have the idea that it takes something artificial to produce happiness. Some people say, "If I had a million dollars, I would be happy." Others say, "If I was elected mayor, or the president of the organization, I would be happy." The answer is, "We must *choose* happiness." We must make it a habit to be happy. It is a mental and spiritual state. Happiness comes through your daily visits with God and in silent communion with His Holy Presence.

Begin now to eat the bread of the silence; you do this by meditating on the fact that, "In Him there is fullness of joy." As you dwell on these words, imagine the joy and the love of God are flowing through your mind and heart as a living current or stream; then you are stirring up the gift of God within you.

Within you is the Power to overcome any situation. You were born to win, to succeed, and to conquer. There is a great thrill in mastering a difficult assignment; the joy is in overcoming. Stand up against the problem now. Take up that shining sword of truth, and say, "I go forth conquering and to conquer!" The Power of the Almighty is within you; It will reveal to you the perfect solution. It will show you the way you should go. Conquer and overcome every negative emotion within you. Love casts out fear. The peace of God casts out pain. Good will casts out envy. In the midst of all kinds of adversity, look for that which is good, and that which is right; in other words look for the Divine answer.

Case Histories

CASE HISTORY NUMBER FOUR

I knew an alcoholic in London who had sunk to the depths of degradation. When I met him, he was begging pennies on the street for drink. At one time he was a highly respected lawyer. I spent some time with him in Hyde Park, London, telling him a few simple truths. I wrote these words for him to repeat: "I surrender myself completely to God and His Boundless Love and Goodness. My mind and heart are now open to the Spirit of Almighty God, which flows through me now. God fills my mind and heart with His Joy and His Love. I do not see the wind, but I feel the breeze upon my face; likewise I feel God's Presence stirring in my heart. God's river of Love flows through me, and I am clean and made whole."

I told him to relax, and slowly articulate the above meditation fifteen minutes, three times a day. All that was necessary was sincerity and humility on his part; then he was assured he would be free from the habit and blessed beyond his wildest dreams. This man became childlike in his simplicity. He fulfilled his promise. In less than a week he was engaged in a romance with God. Truly he touched the hem of His garment. As he meditated aloud, he imagined that the words were seeds sinking down into his soul. On the sixth day his whole being, and his room were flooded with an Interior Light which seemed to blind him temporarily. He was completely healed.

Chapter VI

Harmonious Human Relations

"All things whatsover ye would that men should do unto you, do ye even so to them."

The first thing you learn is that there is no one to change but yourself. The above truth has outer and inner meanings: As you would that men should *think* about you, think you about them in like manner. As you would that men should *feel* about you, feel you also about them in like manner. As you would want men to *act* toward you, act you toward them in like manner. This Biblical passage is the key to happy, human relationships in all walks of life.

Do you observe your "inner talking"? For example, you may be polite and courteous to someone in your office, but when his back is turned, you are very critical and resentful toward him in your mind. Such negative thoughts are highly destructive to you; it is like taking poison; you are actually taking a mental poison that robs you of vitality, enthusiasm, strength, guidance, and good will.

The suggestion you give to the other, you give to yourself. Ask yourself now, "How am I behaving internally toward this other fellow?" This interior attitude is what counts. Begin now to observe yourself; observe your reactions to people, conditions, and circumstances. How do you respond to the events and news of the day? It makes no difference if all the other people were wrong, and you alone were right, if the news disturbs you, it is your evil, because your bad mood affected and robbed you of peace and harmony. You do not have to react negatively to the news or the comments of the broadcaster. You can remain unmoved, undisturbed, and poised, realizing he has a right to his expression and beliefs. It is never what a person says or does that affects us; it is our reaction to what is said or done that matters.

Mentally divide yourself into two people: Your present mental state and that which you desire to be. Look at the thoughts of envy, jealousy, and hatred, which may have enslaved and imprisoned you. You have divided yourself into two people for the purpose of disciplining yourself: One is the race mind working in you, the other is the Infinite or the God-Self seeking expression through you. Be honest with yourself and determine which mood shall prevail.

For example, if someone gossips about you or criticizes you, what is your reaction? Are you going to engage in the typical way by getting excited, resentful, and angry? If you do you are letting the world-mind work in you. You must positively refuse to react in this mechanical, stereotyped, machine-like way. Say positively and definitely to yourself: "The Infinite One thinks, speaks, and acts through me now; this is my Real Self. I now radiate love, peace, and good will to this person who criticized me. I salute the Divinity in him. God speaks through me as peace, harmony, and love. It is wonderful." You are now a real student of truth. Instead of reacting like the herd that returns hate for hate, you have returned love for hatred, peace for hurt, good will for ill will. You have come into truth to think and react in a new way. When you come into truth, you make a new set of reactions to supplant the old. If you find yourself always reacting in the same way to people and conditions, you are not growing. Instead you are standing still, deeply immersed in the conditioned mind.

You know that you do not have to accept negative thoughts. You can become what you want to be by refusing to be a slave to old thought patterns.

Become the real observer, and practice observing your reactions to the events of the day. Whenever you discover that you are about to react negatively, say firmly, "This is not the Infinite One speaking or acting"; this will cause you to stop your negative thinking; then the Divine Love, Light, and Truth will flow through you at that moment. Instead of identifying yourself with anger, resentment, bitterness, and hatefulness, identify immediately with peace, harmony, poise, and balance; with this attitude you are really practicing the art of separation. You are separating yourself from the old (your present, mental state), and you are identifying yourself with the new (that which you desire to be).

Remember this great truth: You do not have to go along with, believe in, nor consent to negative thoughts or reactions. Begin to positively refuse to react mechanically as you formerly did. React and think in a new way. You want to be peaceful, happy, radiant, healthy, prosperous, and inspired; therefore, from this moment forward you must refuse to identify with negative thoughts, which tend to drag you down.

You are the cause of your own anger. If someone called you a fool, why should you get angry? You know you are not a fool. The other person is undoubtedly very disturbed mentally; maybe his child died during the night, or perhaps he is very ill psychologically. You should have compassion on him, but not condemn him. Realize God's peace fills his mind, and that His Love flows through him; then you would be practicing the Golden Rule. You would be identifying not with anger or hatred but with the law of goodness, truth, and beauty.

Would you condemn a person who had tuberculosis? No, you would not. In all probability if he told you, you would realize the Presence of God, harmony, and perfection where the trouble was; that would be compassion. *Compassion* is the Wisdom of God functioning through the mind of man, shown when you forgive all men, and see the God in them.

A person who is hateful, spiteful, envious, and jealous, and who says nasty, mean, scandalous things is very ill psychologically; he is just as sick as the man who has tuberculosis. How are you going to react to such a man? Where is your truth? Where is your wisdom and understanding? Are you going to say, "I am one of the herd; I react in kind; I return spite for spite, hate for hate, and anger for anger?" No, you would stop, and say, "This is not the Infinite One acting through me. God sees only perfection, beauty, and harmony. I see, therefore, as God sees." "Thou art of purer eyes than to behold evil, and canst not look on iniquity." I am going to see all men and women as God sees them. When your eyes are identified with beauty, you will not behold the distorted picture.

You are not living with people, you are living with your concept about them. How are you now responding to John Jones who is next to you on the bench? The fellow who works next to him likes him; his wife loves him; his children think he is wonderful. Perhaps members of his club believe he is generous, kind, and cooperative. Are you thinking of him as mean and petty? Are you resenting him? Who is this fellow? Is he *your* concept, or are all the others wrong? Would it not be wise to look within yourself and determine what it is in you that is causing him to be ugly or a stumbling block to you? I am sure you will find it within yourself.

Maybe you are saying to your son or father when you go home, "That fellow Jones annoys the life out of me. He irritates me beyond words." You are so upset, you cannot digest your dinner properly. According to your description he is impossible.

Where was Jones during the time you were saying all these things? Perhaps he was at the opera with his family; perchance he was out fishing in the stream having a wonderful, glorious time. As a matter of fact if someone said to you, "Where is Jones now?" You would answer, "I do not know." Be honest with yourself now, and admit he is in your own mind as a thought, a concept, or a mental image. You are revealing yourself and your own perturbed state of mind.

Quimby used to say that the suggestion we give to the other, we give to ourselves. You can now see how true that is. As a matter of fact, that is the basis of the Golden Rule. Never suggest to another, or think anything about another, that you would not wish the other to think, suggest, or feel about you.

Watch your hidden conversation to yourself. How do you meet people in your mind when they are thousands of miles away? You may be nice to their face, but the way you think about them is what counts. If you are negative, you are poisoning yourself. There are mental, corrosive poisons, just the same as there are physical, corrosive poisons; they are just as destructive also. If you are now disturbed, agitated, and angry over the way someone has acted toward you, it means you have a very negative thought-pattern in your consciousness, which you should heal instantly.

Be sure that you are not one of those people who will give all the reasons why they should be angry. Stop giving alibis; cease all self-justification. How could you be justified in hating or resenting someone? Do you have a special license? If you do, who gave you this authority? If you are agitated toward another, you are responsible for your unhappiness.

Now you can decree how your thoughts and emotions shall be directed. You are now a king over your own household (mind). Your thoughts, ideas, and feelings are your servants. You issue the command; their mission is to obey. You are here to control, and not to be controlled by angry, wild emotions.

Now when you say to yourself, "Who is the thinker in me?" you must answer, "I am!"

CHAPTER VII

How to Control Your Emotions

The ancient Greeks said, "Man, know thyself." As you study yourself, you seem to be made up of four parts: Your physical body, emotional nature, intellect, and the Spiritual Essence, which is called the Presence of God. The I AM within you, the Divine Presence, is your Real Identity, which is Eternal.

You are here to discipline yourself, so that your intellectual, emotional, and physical nature are completely spiritualized. These four phases of your nature are called the four beasts of *The Book of Revelation*. (*The Revelation of St. John* means God revealing himself as man.)

The real way for you to discipline and bridle your intellectual and emotional nature is by the Practice of the Presence of God all day long.

You have a body; it is a shadow or reflection of the mind. It has no power of itself, no initiative, or volition. It has no intelligence of itself; it is completely subject to your commands or decrees. Look upon your body as a great disc upon which you play your emotions and beliefs. Being a disc, it will faithfully record all your emotionalized concepts and never deviate from them; therefore, you can register a melody of love and beauty, or one of grief and sorrow upon it. Resentment, jealousy, hatred, anger, and melancholia are all expressed in the body as various diseases. As you learn to control your mental and emotional nature, you will become a channel for the Divine, and release the imprisoned splendor that is within you.

Think over this for a moment: You cannot buy a healthy body with all the money in the world, but you can have health through riches of the mind, such as thoughts of peace, harmony, and perfect health.

Let us dwell now on the emotional nature of man. It is absolutely essential for you to control your emotions if you want to grow spiritually. You are considered grown up or emotionally mature when you control your feelings. If you cannot discipline or bridle your emotions, you are a child even though you are fifty years old.

You must remember that the greatest tyrant is a false idea, which controls a man's mind holding him in bondage. The idea you hold about yourself or others induces definite emotions in you. Psychologically speaking, emotions compel you for good or evil. If you are full of resentment toward someone or possessed by a grudge, this emotion will have an evil influence over you, and govern your actions in a manner which has nothing to do with what you say is the original cause. When you want to be friendly and cordial, you will be ugly, cynical, and sour. When you want to be healthy, successful, and prosperous in life, you will find everything going wrong. Those of you reading this book are aware of your capacity to choose a concept of peace and good will. Accept the idea of peace in your mind, and let it govern, control, and guide you.

Quimby pointed out that ideas are our masters, and that we are slaves to the ideas we entertain. The concept of peace with which you now live will induce the feeling of peace and harmony. Your feeling is the Spirit of God operating at the human level; this feeling of peace and goodwill compel you to right action. You are now governed by Divine Ideas, which are mothered by the Holy Spirit.

Uncontrolled or undisciplined emotion is destructive. For example, if you have a powerful automobile, it will take you through the roughest country, or to the top of a high hill; however, you must control the automobile. If you do not know how to drive, you may hit a telegraph pole or another car. Should you step on the gas instead of the brake, the car may be destroyed.

It is wonderful to posses a strong, emotional nature provided you are the master. Your emotions are controlling you if you permit yourself to get angry over trifles or agitated over practically nothing. If you get upset over what you read in the newspapers, you are not controlling your emotions. You must learn to blend your intellect and emotions together harmoniously. The intellect of man is all right in its place, but it should be anointed or illumined with the Wisdom of God.

There are many people who are always trying to intellectualize God. You cannot define the Infinite. Spinoza said that to define God is to deny him. You have met the highly intellectual man who says that man cannot survive death, because he does not take his brain with him. Somehow he is so clever he really believes the brain thinks by itself. Such a man is looking at everything from a three-dimensional standpoint; that is where the intellect ceases.

The intellect, as I said previously, is all right in its place—for example, in our everyday work, and in all kinds of science, art, and industry. However as we approach the Living Spirit Almighty within, we are compelled to leave the world of the intellect, and go beyond into the realm of spiritual values, which are perfection, and where dimension is infinity.

When man's intellect is blended with the emotions of love, peace, and goodwill, he will not use explosives and knowledge of chemistry for the destruction of mankind. The reason man uses the atomic bomb, submarine, and other implements of warfare to destroy his fellow creature is because his spiritual awareness and knowledge lag so far behind his intellectual achievements.

Let us see how emotions are generated. Suppose you observe a cripple; perhaps you are moved to pity. On the other hand you may look at your young, beautiful child, and you feel an emotion of love welling up within you. You know that you cannot imagine an emotion, but if you imagine an unpleasant episode or event of the past, you induce the corresponding emotion. Remember it is essential to entertain the thought first before you induce an emotion.

An emotion is always the working out of an idea in the mind. Have you noticed the effect of fear upon the face, eyes, heart, and other organs? You know the effect of bad news or grief on the digestive tract. Observe the change that takes place when it is found the fear is groundless.

All negative emotions are destructive and depress the vital forces of the body. A chronic worrier usually has trouble with digestion. If something very pleasant occurs in his experience, the digestion becomes normal, because normal circulation is restored, and the necessary gastric secretions are no longer interfered with.

The way to overcome and discipline the emotions is not through repression or suppression. When you repress an emotion, the energy accumulates in the subconscious and remains snarled there. In the same manner as the pressure increases in the boiler, if all the valves are closed, and you increase the heat of the fire, finally there will be an explosion.

Today in the field of psychosomatics we are discovering that many cases of ill health, as arthritis, asthma, cardiac troubles, and failure in life, etc., may be due to suppressed or repressed emotions, perhaps occurring during early life or childhood.

These repressed or suppressed emotions rise like ghosts to haunt you later on. There is a spiritual and psychological way to banish these ghosts, which walk in the gloomy gallery of your mind. The ideal way is the law of substitution. Through the law of mental substitution, you substitute a positive, constructive thought for the negative. When negative thoughts enter your mind, do not fight them; just think of God and His Love; you will find the negative thoughts disappear. "I say unto you, That ye resist not evil." (Math. 5:39) If a person is fearful, the positive emotion of faith and confidence will completely destroy it.

If you sincerely wish to govern your emotions, you must maintain control over your thoughts. By taking charge of your thoughts, you can substitute love for fear. The instant you receive the stimulus of a negative emotion supplant it with the mood of love and good will. Instead of giving way to fear, say, "One with God is a majority." Fill your mind with concepts of peace, love, and faith in God; then the negative thoughts cannot enter.

It is far easier to cremate, burn up, and destroy negative thoughts at the moment they enter the mind, rather than try and dislodge them when they have taken possession of your mind. Refuse to be a victim of negative emotions through controlling your thought and thinking of God and His Attributes. You can be master of all your emotions and conditions. "He that *is* slow to anger is better than the mighty; and he that ruleth his spirit than he that taketh a city."

The Book of Revelation deals with the control of the intellectual and emotional life of man. It says in Chapter 4, verses 6, 7, and 8: "And before the throne *there was* a sea of glass like unto crystal: and in the midst of the throne, and round about the throne, *were* four beasts full of eyes before and behind.

"And the first beasts *was* like a lion, and the second beasts like a calf, and the third beast had a face as a man, and the fourth beast *was* like a flying eagle.

"And the four beasts had each of them six wings about *him;* and *they were* full of eyes within: and they rest not day and night, saying, Holy, holy, holy, Lord God Almighty, which was, and is, and is to come."

The sea of glass before the throne means the inner peace of God, for God is peace. Deep in the centre of your being, the Infinite One lies stretched in smiling repose. It is the Living Presence of God within you. You stand before this throne. *The throne* is a symbol of authority. Your emotional conviction of a deep, abiding faith in the God-Power is your authority in consciousness. To say it simply: Your inner conviction is your throne in heaven, because therein lies your power. "According to your faith it is done unto you." *Faith* is a positive, emotional attitude knowing that the good I seek is mine now.

The four beasts forever before the throne are the four phases of your being: spiritual, mental, emotional, and physical. In order to get your emotional nature on a spiritual basis, it is necessary to understand these four beasts; in doing so you learn the gentle art of scientific prayer which in the final analysis is the answer to all problems. Study these four potencies of consciousness.

The lion is the king of the jungle; it means God, your I AMNESS.

Taurus means the bull or beast of burden. *Your burden* is your desire. You labor in your imagination to make your desire a part of your consciousness.

Aquarius means the water bearer; it means meditation. The word *meditation* means to eat of God or your good, to feast upon your ideal. You pour water on your ideal, meaning you dwell upon and pour love on it, which is the water of life. Something happens as you mentally feast upon your ideal; you generate an emotion; the latter is the spirit of God moving on your behalf. Your emotion is the Holy Spirit moving at human levels. God is a reactive, reciprocal Power within you. Your emotion responds according to the nature of the idea. As you emotionalize your idea, it sinks into the subconscious mind as an impression; this is called the *Eagle* or *Scorpio*, meaning the Divine impregnation. These are the four stages of the unfoldment or manifestation of an ideal or desire. Whatever is impressed is expressed.

The four beasts had each of them six wings. *The six wings* refer to the mental, creative act. When idea and feeling blend together in harmony and faith, there has

taken place a wedding ceremony in the mind. Knowledge of this mental, creative act gives you wings; enables
you to soar aloft above the storms and struggles of the
world, and find peace and strength in your own mind.

Case Histories

CASE HISTORY NUMBER FIVE

A soldier who has returned from Korea told me that
when he was seized with fear, he would say to himself
over and over again, "God's Love surrounds me, and
goes before me." This affirmation impressed his mind
with the feeling of love and faith. This mood of love
supplanted his fear. "Perfect Love casteth out fear." This
procedure is the answer to the process of freedom from
fear.

CASE HISTORY NUMBER SIX

A mother, whose only child died, was grief stricken.
The grief was affecting her vision, and she suffered
from migraine headaches. She was in a deep state of
depression. I suggested to her that she go to a hospital,
and offer her services in the children's ward. She was a
former nurse. In offering her time at a local hospital,
she began to pour out love on the children; she cod-

dled them; cared for them, and fed them. The love was no longer bottled up within her; she became a channel for the Divine, and began to release the sunshine of God's Love. She practiced sublimation, which was a redirection of the energy lodged within her subconscious mind. In this manner she drained off the poison pockets of her subconscious mind.

CASE HISTORY NUMBER SEVEN

A woman who comes to our meeting told me that she was accustomed to fits of temper and anger periodically by the action of neighbors. Instead of letting the anger and hatred affect her mentally and physically by pushing it back into the subconscious, she transmuted it into muscular energy by getting a gallon of water and washing the windows or the floor. Sometimes she would begin to dig in the garden, saying to herself aloud, "I am digging in the garden of God, and planting God's ideas." She would do this for fifteen minutes at a time. When washing the windows, she would say aloud, "I am cleansing my mind with the waters of love and life." The above illustrations are simple methods of working off negative emotions in a physical way.

CHAPTER VIII

Changing the Feeling of "I"

If you say, "I," to everything you think, feel, say, or imagine, you cannot transform your emotional life. Remember all kinds of thoughts can enter your mind; all kinds of emotions may enter your heart. If you say, "I," to all negative thoughts, you are identifying yourself with them, and you cannot separate internally from them. You can refuse to attach "I" to negative emotions and thoughts. You make it a practice to avoid muddy places as you walk along the road; likewise you must avoid walking down the muddy roads of your mind where fear, resentment, hostility, and ill-will lurk and move. Refuse to listen to negative remarks. Do not touch the negative moods, or let them touch you. Practice inner separation by getting a new feeling about yourself, and about what you really are. Begin to realize that the real "I" in you is the Infinite Spirit, the Infinite One.

Begin to identify yourself with the Qualities and Attributes of this Infinite One; then your whole life will be transformed. The whole secret in transforming your negative, emotional nature is to practice self-observation. To observe and *to observe* oneself are two different things. When you say, "You observe . . ." you mean you give your attention to external things. In self-observation the attention is directed inwards. A man may spend his whole lifetime studying the atom, stars, body, and the phenomenalistic world—namely, knowledge of the external world; this knowledge cannot bring about an interior change. Self-observation is the means of interior change—the change of the heart. You must learn to differentiate, to discern, to separate the chaff from the wheat.

You practice the art of self-observation when you begin to ask yourself, "Is this idea true? Will it bless, heal, and inspire me? Will it give me peace of mind, and contribute to the well-being of humanity?" You are living in two worlds: the external and the internal; yet they are both one. One is visible and the other invisible (subjective and objective). Your external world enters through your five senses, and is shared by everyone. Your internal world of thought, feelings, sensations, beliefs, and reaction is invisible and belongs to you. Ask yourself, "In which world do I live? Do I live in the world revealed by my five senses, or in this inner world?" It is in this inner world you live all the time; this is where you feel and suffer. Suppose you are invited to a banquet. All you see, hear, taste, smell, and touch belong to the external world. All that you think, feel, like, and dislike belong to the inner world. You attend two banquets recorded differently: namely, one the outer, and one the inner. It is in your inner world of thought, feeling, and emotion in which you rise and fall and sway to and fro.

In order to transform yourself, you must begin to change the inner world through the purification of the emotions, and the correct ordering of the mind through right thinking. If you want to grow spiritually, you must transform yourself. *Transformation* means the changing of one thing into another.

In order truly to observe yourself, you must see that regardless of what happens, your thought and feeling are fixed on this great truth: "How is it in God and Heaven?" This will lift you up, and transform all your negative thoughts and emotions. You may be inclined to say that other people are to blame, because of the way they talk or act, but if what they say or do makes you negative, you are inwardly disturbed; this negative state is where you now live, move, and have your being.

P.D. Ouspensky used to point out that people became upset easily, because their feeling of "I" was derived from negative states of consciousness. The feeling of "I" was one of his favorite expressions, and some of his ideas are incorporated in this chapter.

When you say, "I think this . . ." "I think that . . ." "I resent this . . ." or "I dislike this . . ." which "I" is speaking? Is it not a different "I" speaking every moment? Each "I" is completely different. One "I" in you criticizes one moment; a few minutes later another "I" speaks tenderly. Look at and learn about your different "I's," and know deep within yourself that certain "I's" will never dominate, control, or direct your thinking.

Take a good look at the "I's" you are consorting with. With what kind of people do you associate? I am referring to the people that inhabit your mind. Remember your mind is a city; thoughts, ideas, opinions, feelings, sensations, and beliefs dwell there. Some of the places in your mind are slums and dangerous streets; however Jesus (your savior) is always walking down the streets of your mind in the form of your ideal, desire, and aim in life.

One of the meanings of Jesus is your desire; for your desire, when realized, is your savior. Your aims and objectives in life are now beckoning to you; move toward them. Give your desire your attention; in other words take a lively interest in it. Go down the streets of love, peace, joy, and good will in your mind; you will meet wonderful people on the way. You will find beautifully lighted streets and wonderful citizens on the better streets of your mind.

Never permit your house, which is your mind, to be full of servants that you do not have under control. When you were young, you were taught not to go with what your mother called, "bad company." Now when you begin to awaken to your inner powers, you must make it a special point that you do not go with wrong "I's" (thoughts) within you.

I had an interesting chat with a young man who studied mental discipline in France. His procedure was to take, as he said, "mental photographs of himself from time to time." He would sit down, and think about his emotions, moods, thoughts, sensations, reactions, and his tones of voice; then he would say, "These are not of God; they are false. I will go back to God and think from that Standard or Rock of Truth." He practiced the art of inner separation. He would stop when he got angry, and say, "This is not the Infinite One, the real 'I' speaking, thinking, or acting; it is the false 'I' in me."

Return to God like this young man. Every time you are prone to get angry, critical, depressed, or irritable, think of God and Heaven, and ask yourself, "How is it in God and Heaven?" *There* is the answer to becoming the new man; this is how you become spiritually reborn or experience what is called the second birth. (*The second birth* is internal discipline and spiritual understanding.)

The saint and the sinner are in all of us; so are the murderer and the holy man; likewise are God and the world mind. Every man basically and fundamentally wants to be good, to express good, and to do good. This is "the positive" in you. If you have committed destructive acts, as for example, if you have robbed, cheated, and defrauded others, and they condemn you, and they hold you in a bad light, you can rise out of the slum of your mind to that place in your own consciousness where you cease to condemn yourself; then all your accusers must still their tongues. When you cease to accuse yourself, the world will no longer accuse you; this is the power of your own consciousness; It is the God in you.

The other self represents the many "I's" in you, for instance the many negative ideas and beliefs that there are powers outside your own consciousness; the belief that others can hurt you; the elements are unfriendly, plus the fears, superstitions, and ignorance of all kinds. Finally prejudices, fears, and hates drive and goad you to do that which you would not otherwise do. The ideal way to change the feeling of "I" is to affix to the real "I" within you everything that is noble, wonderful, and God-like.

Begin to affirm, "I am strong. I am radiant. I am happy. I am inspired. I am illumined. I am loving. I am kind. I am harmonious." Feel these states of mind; affirm them, and believe them; then you will begin to truly live in the Garden of God. Whatever you affix to the "I AM" and believe, you become. The "I AM" in you is God, and there is none other. "I AM" or Life, Awareness, Pure Being, Existence, or the Real Self of you is God. It is the Only Cause. It is the Only Power making anything in the world. Honor It.

ABOUT THE AUTHORS

JOSEPH MURPHY was born in 1898 on the southern coast of Ireland. Raised in a devout Catholic family, Murphy had planned on joining the priesthood. As a young man he instead relocated to America to make his career as a chemist and druggist. After running a pharmacy counter at New York's Algonquin Hotel, Murphy began studying mystical and metaphysical ideas. In the 1940s he became a popular New Thought minister and writer. Murphy wrote prolifically on the autosuggestive and mystical faculties of the human mind. He became widely known for his metaphysical classic, *The Power of Your Subconscious Mind*, which has sold millions of copies since it first appeared in 1963. Considered one of the pioneering voices of New Thought and affirmative-thinking philosophy, Murphy died in Laguna Hills, California, in 1981.

MITCH HOROWITZ is the PEN Award-winning author of books including *Occult America* and *The Miracle Club*. A writer-in-residence at the New York Public Library and lecturer-in-residence at the University of Philosophical Research in Los Angeles, Mitch introduces and edits G&D Media's line of Condensed Classics and is the author of the Napoleon Hill Success Course series, including *The Miracle of a Definite Chief Aim* and *The Power of the Master Mind*. Visit him at MitchHorowitz.com.

Printed in the USA
CPSIA information can be obtained
at www.ICGtesting.com
JSHW012044140824
68134JS00033B/3250